WIFE OR NO WIFE IN LIFE

Wife or no Wife in Life

My Wife And You

Live As My Wellwisher

My Uncle And The Ghost

Ambitious

Turning Point

Durga Prasad

Price ₹ 199

To My Wife

Smt. Basanti Devi - "The Woman Behind His Success."

Index

S.No.	Title	Page No.
1	Wife or no Wife in Life	3
2	My Wife And You	15
3	Live as my Wellwisher	22
4	My Uncle And The Ghost	30
5	Ambitious	47
6	Turning Point	61

WIFE OR NO WIFE IN LIFE

Wife is a wonderful word we know about. It can be defined as an important part of one's life (Here one's life means the life of a man).
Wife is a woman married with a man having equal role to play with or equal right and duty to share with particularly with so called husband and generally with the people so called the members of the family which she belongs to for some specific reason or cause.
Wife is an important part and parcel of family and thus she has to perform her duty to please everybody with due love and affection, honour and respect, care and courtesy and so on. She is entrusted with household work which she has to perform sincerely for the peace, pleasure and prosperity of the family as a whole without any discrimination and disparity.

Wife is also known as better half which is used normally by better full (Here I mean to say better husband).

I have never tried to consult any dictionary whether "better full" word is there or not. I have gone through the chapter of gender and came across numerous words which are masculine. Normally masculine gender has got its feminine gender. For instance husband is masculine gender and its feminine gender is wife. Similarly brother to sister, father to mother, uncle to aunt, dog to bitch, horse to mare, bull to cow, king to queen etc. The feminine gender appears quite different from its masculine gender in appearance. In human beings we can distinguish or differentiate the moment we see her, look at her, talk to her and so on but it is too difficult to recognize a male from a female in case of birds, a few beasts and insects like cockroach, spider, lizard, scorpion etc. Some domestic animals who usually live with us like cow, bull, he-goat, she goat, dog, bitch, he-hare, she hare, cock, hen, horse , mare, buffalo, donkey can be recognized whether male or female the moment we see their appearance. Male and female differ each other in so many things in behavior in look and in appearance.

There is no wrong if better full is used for husband inasmuch as better half is used for wife.

Most of the men in and around the world have their wives, only a few remain (Here remain means live and lead life without wives) bachelors, they don't marry, why so? The reason is best known to such people but there must be some specific reasons for remaining bachelors. I have never made research over this subject till now as to why people do not marry. I can guess the reasons whether I am correct or not it is up to you to judge. There is a condition for participation in the debate i.e. he must be a bachelor – it is one part of the coin – let it be a head and the other part of it – let it be a tail in case such persons are women. In fact let its percentage be minimal, some women also remain bachelor I mean to say they do not marry. Here also there lies some specific reasons but who can approach such women and can ask them the reasons why they do not marry in life. it is logically accepted phenomenon that there is always an answer to a question. Only presumption or assumption can help to some extent. Over and above the autobiography or biography or life history of such men or women can be helpful to us to know the exact reasons of not marrying. Why women do not marry will be covered in the next story. Now let us concentrate on men only.

The reasons of remaining bachelors (Not marrying) are summarized as follows:

Why men marry: It's quite obvious that to fulfil the physiological excitement or provocation, willingness or desire or impulse or force or compulsion or need or requirement so to say food and drink alike people marry woman.

It's the first and foremost reason that most of the men marry women. The moment the people reach the age of puberty, the sex organs are stimulated internally and disturb mentally in such a way that they do not feel comfortable in any way unless or until they do sex with women.

Secondly for family the people marry so that their dynasty/generation can continue for the years to come one after another.

Those who do not marry are afraid of losing most of the valuables like their relatives, kith and kin, their friends and associates, space of time, vision and goal, aim and objective and the last but not the least masculinity, power, freedom and so on.

In India these people didn't marry. Once we look into their autobiography or biography we may know the reasons why they didn't marry in life:

1. **Swami Dayanand Saraswati:** He wanted to do something great in life.
   He gave up the idea of marrying someone as he accepted sannyasa. He was in search of a Guru and found in Vijayanand Saraswati all qualities of Guru. Though his Guru was blind but was the master of Indian lore. He made up his mind not to indulge in worldliness for the objective wouldn't be achieved in life what he had thought of. He founded Arya Samaj and did numerous social and religious reforms. He is considered one of the greatest religious leaders ever born in India. He was born on 12th. February 1824 and died on 30th. October 1883. He was a profound scholar of the Vedic lore and had mastery over Sanskrit language and literature.

2 Swami Vivekanand: He didn't marry. He was well aware of the fact that once he married, he wouldn't be able to contribute to the people of the society what he had thought of. He established Hinduism, its religion, tradition and culture and so on the universal platform. So far as I learn while after finishing his world famous speech in Chicago, America in September 1893 at the Parliament of the World's Religions, the participants and the people of the world were extremely impressed and a lady – a social worker, author and teacher was so influenced by him that she proposed Swami Vivekanand.to become his disciple. Swami Ji agreed to it provided she wanted to live with him as sister. She was convinced and agreed to live with him as sister and since then Swami Ji started calling her **Bhagini Nivedita.** In Bengali literature Bhagini means sister.

Once Swami Ji said, "Great work is done only with great sacrifice."

3 Vinoba Bhave: Vinoba Bhave didn't marry in life as he dedicated his whole life

For the welfare of downtrodden landless people of the country. He was the founder of the Bhoodan Movement and for that he travelled various states on foot and asked the privileged people of the society to donate their lands for the landless. He is considered as a National Teacher of India and the spiritual successor of Mohandas Gandhi.

He was born on 11 September 1895 in a small village of Raigad District of Maharashtra. His earlier name was Vinayaka Rao Bhave. He was a freedom fighter. He took active part in struggle for freedom of the nation and jailed several times. He did so many religious and social work for the needy people. He walked on foot all over the country for 13 years and set up 6 ashrams beside Brahma Vidya Mandir. He studied the Bhagwat Gita and wrote religious and spiritual books too. He left for heavenly abode on 15 November 1982. He is also known as Acharya Vinoba Bhave. After death he was bestowed the highest civilian award of India " Bharat Ratna " in 1983 by the then President of India. He was the true disciple of Mahatma Gandhi and followed him truly for the cause of humanity. A rare personality of simplicity and generosity of the nation with depth of spiritual knowledge and religious thought.

4 Atal Bihari Vajpayee: He didn't marry because he didn't get the time. When somebody questioned him and wanted to know the reason of not marring. Jokingly or seriously he replied, "I did not get the time even to think over this issue in life. He meant to say he was too busy to work in politics for the welfare of mankind. He reached to the top position of the country and did a lot. He served the nation in various capacities and lastly retired as Prime Minister of India. He is reckoned as **"Ajatshatru"** meaning thereby he has no enemy.

5 APJ Abdul Kalam: Why he didn't marry is

still a secret as nobody knows the exact reason for not marrying, but as it is obvious he has dedicated himself physically, mentally and spiritually to space research – the only aim that he had fixed up early in life. It is no exaggeration to say that he has sacrificed for the cause of progress and prosperity of the country's power in the field of space engineering, science and technology.

6 Sri Sri Ravi Shankar: He didn't marry as has dedicated his life for spreading spirituality and its quality and role in human life. It is the spirituality that brings forth peace and harmony in one's life and only then one can be happy and gay otherwise not at all. He is the founder of "Art of Living" and teaches that spirituality is that which enhances human values such as love and affection, mercy and compassion, inspiration and enthusiasm. He is also known as spiritual leader all over the world

.7 Baba Ramdev: Everybody knows why Baba Ramdev didn't marry in life. So many times people asked him why he didn't marry. He replied with smile, "I joined Gurikul at early age and dedicated from there itself my life for yoga and Aurveda. Once decided, decided for ever not to marry." All of us are well aware of what Baba Ramdev has been giving to the people of India and beyond that all over the world – a unique and superb methodology to remain fit and healthy whole life with no cost.

It is his contribution that yoga is recognised, accepted and honoured almost all over the countries of the world and due to that 21st. June is declared the world Yoga Day by UNO and moreover the day is celebrated enthusiastically by world community. Indian Government came forward and did a lot for its recognition worldwide.

The percentage of such people in society is minimal even though it is the outcome of the sacrifice that the people make to remain bachelor throughout their lives and contribute virtually what the society needs to flourish like anything. The reasons attributable to the issue of not marrying is crystal clear that a few people do not marry as they have some specific aim or objective to achieve or fulfil. Such people are of the opinion that once they marry, they will lose freedom and as such they fail to achieve in life what they have thought of.

There is a very popular quote the people use to say: "To marry a woman is just like Delhi's laddoo (A kind of sweets) whosoever has eaten it has to repent and whosoever has not eaten it has to repent too."

****

My WIFE AND YOU

I do not know how she (not my wife but somebody else) came to know that I'm an author, may be possible she might have read some of my love short stories in net or website.

Yesterday late in the morning at about 11 I got a call from some foreign country (I knew it later on but I don't like to disclose – "Raj ko raj rahne do - let the secret remain as secret"). The unfortunate part of this story now begins with as introduction is that that my wife was present and engaged in sewing her so called blouse (She is not only my better half but a better tailor also).

She starts – "I'm Sophia, talking from Colombia."

What's the matter, Mrs. Sophia?

I wanted to talk to you face to face in leisure, now I'm free, no work, all disposed of, and sitting shy, feeling monotony.

O, I see! What can I do for you, Mrs. Sophia?

Please favour me with your Email ID, I want to mail you and ask you about the love short stories you write these days. I gonna almost all such stories available in net or site.

Then why don't you want my mail ID?

It's paying though small amount but can't pay every time. I request you to mail me a copy as a good friend of mine the moment it is published somewhere.

O.k.

Mr. Prasad! You are a nice man.

I switched off my smart phone to avoid the ensuing tsunami.

My wife was listening the conversation though one side but trying to know that of the other side.

Who is he talking so long?

I don't know.

Telling a lie.

Not at all. Swearing for God's sake.

The way you were inclined to talk to, he must be a woman not a man.

What of that?

Just then she called me again.

Disrupted, so couldn't finish … ?

Mr. Prasad ! You're a nice gentleman.

How did you conclude we never saw each other, we never be face to face, we never peeped into eyes each other, we never loved each other…

Obviously we love each other, if you not, then be sure and certain I.

Amazing!

I see you in your every short love story – I see you the roll you play as an actor and characterize the hero of the story – unbeaten, unmatched and what not..?

As my wife was staring at me with her burning eyes, I switched off once again but after a few minutes she called me again.

Mr. Prasad! You are a very (This time she used an adjective before man) nice man.

Let me confess to satisfy you but I'm not a nice man in the eyes of my wife.

My wife listening this absurd comment about her jumped upon me like a lioness.

What did you utter about me?

Nothing.

Nothing? I'll teach you at …?

Let me finish, then you have liberty to do with me whatever you like - can scold me, can abuse me and even … I can bear all as usual.

On the other side she (The lady) was listening to our talk.

She asked me," I heard some harsh voice.

It's my wife's. You love me. Isn't it?

Of course!

In fact whosoever come in contact with me start loving me, how can I stop anybody in doing so?

But your wife? She questioned me with a sheer surprise.

She didn't at all. She is of the opinion and she set it in her mind that I love women other than her, inclined to them the moment I come into contact or be in touch with anyone.

Mr. Prasad! Truly speaking I ... I too don't love my husband rather I hate him.

The reason?

The reason is almost the same.

Please clarify.

Whenever he sees any woman in person or talks to over phone, he starts inclining as if she were everything and I am nothing.

Mr. Prasad! All wives are more or less of the same nature or attitude.

Please suggest me as a good wife the best solution to this problem.

Here is for you and all concerned:

The only way - so to say solution is to keep silent and bear with whatever your wife comments. I'm sanguine she will be calm and cool after a short time. That is why the wife is termed as better half. Nothing left out for me to explain further.

Any practical instance that I can share with you with ease.

Whenever my husband sees any woman or talks to any woman over telephone, I reacted – not only I scold but abuse and even threaten to divorce. At that time when I am at the top of my voice, he keeps calm and quit and bears with sheer patience.

Mr. Prasad! The another part of the coin is much more interesting… ?

So curios she made me that I intervened to know immediately.

What is that other part?

After a short interval I stand up, catch hold of my husband under my arms and you know I kiss him – one after another… long enough.

Gracias ! I thanked her in Spanish language.

Adios ! She switched off her smart phone saying good bye in Spanish language in turn.

You know what my wife did after that ... She repeated the same thing.

****

Live As My Well – wisher

It is said that one cannot forget his/her first love throughout his or her life. I am sanguine that those whosoever would have fallen in love at first sight in childhood or boyhood, most probably in school or college with a girl or boy, he/she recollects the sweet – sweet days spent together hands in hands, under the arms, eyes to eyes fathoming into depth of hearts all along, gossiping about love and romance for hours together in a lonely place far from the worldliness.

Love at this age is quite different – sex is almost far – far away from the awareness of what sex means and how can be indulged in and can be enjoyed together. The sex organs/limbs are either not developed or in an in – matured stage. But one thing is quite clear that there is attraction to each other , there is sensation in cell , there is emotion in whole body , and over and above there is restlessness to see each other , to meet probably alone ,to talk face to face , to touch and embrace frequently in emotion and so on … ?

All such things happen gradually with pace of time – mean to say when they are grown up – in man moustaches start appearing on the upper lip and beard grows on and around the chin whereas in woman breast begins to rise upward. In man semen starts coming out whereas in woman menses takes place. Face indicates youthfulness all around in man and woman both. Most of the people don't have the courage to disclose their first love for incident took place in his school or college life long back. They conceal it or hesitate to speak out anything about the past. They prefer either to forget or like to preserve it in mind. It is not good at all to keep it in Pandora's box as it has got some side effect on body and in mind as well.

One of my friends took me in his car to Shakti Mandir in the evening. There we sat for hours

together in meditation. At the exit he introduced me to a lady – very beautiful even at 50, well dressed in pink sari and blouse, long black hair – in a single choti to her buttock – sparking eyes – slightly bigger too, a red bindi on her forehead, juicy lips , a garland of white pearls around the neck – all together she looked charming . My friend at the first sight lost his balance and caught hold of her left hand in filmy style and said :
Shalu , Tum ! (You) , Kab aayee ? (When did you come ?)

She recollected, stared at him and suddenly responded , ' Gopal ! Tum, after such a long time, I see you have not changed at all – same look, same face, same hair style and so on … I came yesterday on the eve of Rakhi Poornima . How are you ? How is Bhabhi Jee ? Your children ? Uncle and aunt Jee?

Father is no more. Mother suffers from blood sugar and blood pressure. Wife is fatty, not slim like you. Savita is in USA with her husband. She is a software engineer, her husband too. Rohit after MBA is looking after my business. We have Hero Honda Agency. Me not well .

"Why? You very often come in my dreams. And my blood burns whenever I remember you – your immense love and particularly the pleasant moment spent and enjoyed together. I have never thought of it that you would be married to someone else the moment I left for Mumbai for study law. I have everything but nothing. Why nothing? You know we had decided to marry but my dad knowing about our love affairs sent me to Mumbai to study law. Your dad arranged your marriage immediately on my dad's persuasion. What happened later, you know better . Me too . I refused to marry someone whom I did not know at all.

I declared that I would marry as per my choice, but my mother forced me to obey my father and marry the groom gladly he had already selected.

Finding no way out to protest, I had to surrender to the situation ultimately. My mum was a heart patient. She wanted me to obey my father otherwise she would breathe her last."

Turning to me Gopal said to her, ' He is Mr. Kailash, my fast friend . He consoles me time to time whenever heart beat fluctuates while remembering you. Shalu ! I can't forget you though I have become Dada – Nana . I have told everything about you to my wife. Even my children know about you and our love. If I would not have told them, I would have left for heavenly abode long back. Let us sit in a café and have coffee together.

As you like, I have no objection.

We came to Madras Café.

"Those days you liked onion masala dosa. Isn't it?"

"Of course."

Gopal ordered for onion masala dosa , sada dosa for us. Gopal asked, ' How are you these days, your husband , your children , your business ?

"My husband is an LIC agent, myself a teacher in a Girls' High School. Three daughters – all married, one son, competed NDA, now in training in Pune. Only two members are left, we live together happily.

Do you remember me?

Not always but kabhi – kabhi .

Still do you love me?

Please don't ask such a question from a married Indian woman. In fact I can't reply. My husband loves me most. He trusts me also. I cannot think about any unusual thing like this after marriage. I cannot betray him. I was very open to you and now also. In the first night of honey moon we didn't sleep, we exchanged our views about our past life. He disclosed that he had a girlfriend whom he had loved, kissed and even had intercourse .Now none is even in his dream after marriage. Have you any boy friend with whom …? – All of a sudden he asked me . I replied confidently, 'Not at all. I disliked such things before marriage.' Here I told a lie because once you warned me not to disclose anything to anyone even to my husband in case not married to you about the love affair I had had with you otherwise I would be in trouble, whole life I would have to shed tears and had to repent as no husband would like that his wife would have had some illicit relationship with someone before marriage. My husband persuaded me on many occasions in tactful manner but I always convinced him that I was never entangled with any one as my family culture and tradition didn't permit it before one's marriage. Gopal ! I am very grateful to you for your valuable suggestion; otherwise my life would have become a hell instead of a heaven.

Alright. I want you to spare a few hours for me.

Gopal ! I understand what you want, but practically after marriage for a woman like me, it is not possible. It is against social ethics. If you want anything else other than this, even my life, I can give you. If I do so, I will be of nowhere. Please excuse me for God's sake. Forget it for ever. Live and lead life as my well – wisher.

Shalini thanked us for company and left hastily. Gopal was at a loss to decide where to go then? Even the hell was houseful.

****

Gouri Shankar, My Uncle and the Ghost

My uncle Gouri Shankar was a very dare devil person to go even to the places where ghosts were living with their family for a pretty long time more than five hundred years or so. How he became so courageous was a mystery. But a time came when that mystery was broken into pieces and everyone came to know that he had learnt some mantras to bind his body with it before approaching the ghostly areas. It was well known to everybody once the body was bound with the mantra, no ghost could harm, couldn't touch even. People believed so.

Early in the morning we used to leave our beds and left for the field to play football. There was a very good football ground in Gobindpur, my village and the senior players used to play and practice every evening.

GFC was known to one and all for excellent performance in the football maches in the district and the state as well.

We were well aware of the information, the dates, the days and the time too when our seniors didn't play in the evening. We preferred to play that day/date in the evening.
Football play in the evening is considered the most appropriate time. So we utilized the ground for our purposes.

I kept watch on my uncle and his movement and whereabouts.

I very often noticed and found his bed was vacant, only was covered with pillows properly with long bed sheet thereon.

I never minded. But curiosity compelled me to know where he went so early in the morning alone. Those days in 1958 when I was merely 13 years old and I was reading in class IX in Gobindpur High School. I used to read mostly detective books and as such I wanted to become captain Hamid one of the famous characters in the detective books of Ibne Safi B.A. Those were the days when such books were available for merely Rs.2/3 or so. There was a big library known as Vani Mandir in the first floor and my class friend Kali Shaw was the librarian. A statue of The Goddess of learning was installed in the ground floor every year on the eve of Basant Panchmi and the students of the locality used to worship her with sheer love, respect and enthusiasm.

The library contained a large collection of books of different subjects and categories. I got a golden opportunity to read books free of cost. Though there was strict rule to issue one book at a time to a member but Kali Shaw issued me two books at a time one in my name and another in his name.

BN Gupta popularly known as Bhola Babu was an efficient and wise man. Due to his extra ordinary quality and ability he was closely associated to the Dy. Commissioner of Dhanbad. He was very near and dear to him.

So our library was granted some aids also regularly to buy books that enriched it beside it enriched the knowledge of the people too.

So far as I remember the then Dy. Commissioner of Dhanbad was very fond of English books and very often used to visit AH Wheeler & Co. book stall in the second platform of Dhanbad Station.

I also used to go there to buy some books of my choice in Hindi as well as in English. I saw DC Saheb selecting only English books himself. He had had body guard and orderly with him all the time.

The people of the district and nearby places had donated those books on the call of the then Deputy Commissioner and the Head Clerk, BN Gopta, the resident of my village. The parents were against us reading of any books other that what were prescribed in the curriculum. At the prime age of youth some books of Kushwaha Kant and Pyarelal Awara were very interesting for us to read. These books were rarely available but Kali Shaw kept for me. We made up our mind to collect money and then to buy them secretly. I read some detective books in English too from the library and buying from the station as well. I did so for a pretty long time. I liked to read Sarat Da's Srikant, Devdas, Grihda, bankim Babu's Anand Math, Prem Chand's Godan, Nirmala, short stories – Pus Ki Raat, Kafan, Panch Parmeshwar etc. Renu's Maila Aanchal, Dhanjal rinjal, Tisri Kasam etc. In English "The old Man and the Sea" by Earnest Hemingway influenced my life to a great extent. As you like, The Merchant of Venice, The Taming of the Shrew, As you like it by William Shakespeare enriched my knowledge of English language and literature. The short stories of Chekhov, O Henri, Maupassant etc. were my favourites.

I buy some of good monthly magazines – Sarika, Navneet, Kadambini, Sarita, Manohar Kahaaniyan, Dharmyug, Filmfare etc. for myself and for Ayodhya Babu. My friend was a business man and bought the Awaj, the Aryavart and the Indian Nation. I read them as and when I happened to see him regularly in his floor mill.

I followed my uncle one day and found him entering the house of Hargori Shaw. I was more surprised than ever as to how my uncle came in contact with the veteran Tantric.

I knew all about my uncle's regular visit to him and concluded that he had become his disciple and learning mantras to bind his body and also to persuade ghosts.

Hargori Shaw was so popular in the village that as and when people used to see him for some tantric vidya.

His popularity spread all around when he spent the whole night alone in the funeral ghat of Khudia River where at midnight ghosts along with some women quite -- ? – with brooms in their hands used to dancing and rejoicing the moment like anything. Those were the days the people were believing it and the same time very afraid of going there with the fall of day.

As my uncle was a vagabond, no control over him and even my grandmother was afraid of him particularly when he threatened her that if she said anything against what he did, he would have no way out but to flee away from the house and then she would have to repent over whole life.

It was mere coincidence that that Hargori Shaw came and sat on the small chouki beside me. He asked my friend who was looking after his floor mill to grind the wheat first and give him as he had to go sharp to nearby village where a man was attacked by some ghost and the man was so strong and stout that he was out of control by the villagers.

"Let me grind my friend's wheat first, then I will do yours." my friend said to him.

He looked and stared at me with burning eyes and I too with making my faces that I was not afraid of him and his mantra.

He wanted me to forego my turn and allow him in fear to grind his floor earlier than me.

My friend heard our conversation and hinted me not to be harsh against Hargori Babu, better allow him to get the floor. I kept mum and my friend ground his wheat on priority basis and gave his bag

My uncle addressed Hargori Babu as uncle. I addressed him as Hargori Dada.

Hargori Dada was very popular due to his peculiar personality. He was of about 45 years old, strong and stout, a big head with big eyes and flatted nose, dense beard and moustache, hairs on upper ears, thick neck. The hairs on the head was long but tied properly in knots.

As I came to know he had no family. He had an elder brother who rarely lived with him.

Both brothers had landed property in the distant village where his elder brother used to live most of the time with his family.

There were different stories the elderly people very often said and shared for the sake of excitement or entertainment.

Some people said that Hargori Dada at 17 came in contact with a tantric of Kamru - Kamkhya, Assam and so much more influenced than ever that he left home and returned after a long period. During the period of stay in Kamru – Kamkhya he learnt so many magic, tantra-mantra etc.

One story that drew my attention is that the women were so versed in magical feat that they could convert the handsome men into sheep in day and at night converted them into men and for what I came to know when I became young enough to understand all such things.

I heard people saying, "Don't quarrel with Hargoriya, otherwise, if he is displeased or annoyed, he will convert into sheep. He is Kamru-Kamkhya returned."

Jokingly or seriously some people pointed it out in jealousy that he was already married in childhood and brought his wife on return from Kamru-Kamkhya. One midnight, when he was gossiping with his wife, he tested his mantra to convert her into a sheep. No sooner did he sprinkle magical water over his wife's head than she changed into a sheep. He tried to convert the sheep into a woman but in vain. He became so nervous that finding no way out, he took the sheep to his guru to Assam to change it into a woman but unfortunately his guru was not traced out in spite of searching so many places. He handed over the sheep to a woman whom he trusted and requested her to see his guru to convert the sheep into a woman and if it was done, immediately to inform him over trunk call or drop a postcard.

After a few years Hargori Dada came to know that his guru took the sheep away with him and what happened after that none intimated him. Since then Hargori Dada led a lonely life. He was quite aloof or cut off from the worldliness. He cursed himself and his guru too.

Nobody was knowing what job he was doing and how he was earning his bread.

One thing was crystal clear that people of Gobindpur were paying him due respect and also extending assistance in need.

My uncle came to know that I had seen him talking to Hargori Dada.

He threatened me for dire consequences if I disclosed it to his mother. Consequently I kept mum over that issue.

My uncle was married at early age. His Sasural was at Pradhankhanta nearly 3 miles from our house. There was a kachcha narrow road from Gobindpur to Baliapur via Pradhankhanta. Just after 2 miles from Gobindpur there is village namely Jagdish and at the lowest level of the road there is a Joriya following from the Dhangi Mountain. Above the Joriya (A small river alike) a huge area is covered with rocky land inside which the elderly people state that there is big dwelling place for the ghosts who live there with their family for a pretty long time happily. Normally they come out any time in the evening and at midnight.

After 6 years my uncle brought my aunt from Pradhankhanta. It is termed as Gouna or Diviragaman in Bihar and UP custom or tradition or culture.

My aunt's father was a very rough and tough man by nature. After three days my aunt's brother came and took her with him.

My grandmother sent my uncle many a time to bring his wife but his Sasurji turned down his request every time, the reason best known to him.

My uncle went to his Sasural to see my aunt every now and then on bicycle in the morning and coming back before the Sun set.

But one day his father-in-law was out of station, so he stayed there in Sasural for a longer period late in the evening. Here in our house my grandmother was worried about my uncle and was coming out of the house off and on to see anxiously whether her son had come. She sent Bisna our servant to go to Pradhankhanta and to find out as to why he was late in returning.

Bisna left on bicycle as ordered by my grandmother immediately. After an hour at dark night I saw my uncle hanging under the arms of mussel men and coming back but in a furious state of mind.

I noticed his legs and hands were tied up tightly by strong rope. My uncle was trying to get rid of the tie but in vain.

My grandmother was stunned to find his son in such an unexpected state. My uncle was abusing all in filthy language.

Hari Singh, a muscleman of my grandmother' parents, turned his face and said to my grandmother the whole story in brief.

People outside the house said, "Gourishankra ke bhut lag gayeel Ba, Jagdish ke jodiyaa men." (The ghost has entered his body and mind of Gouri Shankar at Jagdish river.)

The news spread like jungle fire all around the village and the people of all ages, caste and community started surrounding my house to see the ghost who had entered my uncle's body and had captured not only his whole body and mind but empowered it and saying his name and the place from where he had come. Now my uncle appeared to be very strong man and not allowing anybody to touch his body even. He was so furious like carnivorous animal that he began attacking the people who made faces to him. All such problems took place when my grandmother asked Hari Singh to untie the knots and to let him free. He was not recognising his own mother. He used filthy languages the moment she approached him and said affectionately, " Son! my dear son! What wrong have I done that you are abusing me in front of so many people? "

My uncle jumped upon her and caught her by her hair – knot. He wanted to throw her on the ground but Hari Singh pushed him out.

Hari Singh called Sitaram Dada who was knowing some mantra to control ghost and to sweep away from the haunted body. Sitaram Dada came and asked for some yellow mustard seeds and mustard oil. My grandmother went inside the kitchen and brought the same. Sitaram Dada recited some holy mantras and threw the seeds over my uncle's body. My uncle caught hold of Sitaram Dada under his arms and supressing from all sides. He was also abusing, " Madhad…! Tatric banta hai , sab --- men ----

denge, samjha hai kya , salaalaa!, haraamjaadaa! , haramkhor! Chal hat , aaj chod diya , mama samajhkar, agar koyee dusra hota to gardaniye machod dete."

Sitaram Mama was trembling in fear. He said clearly to his sister, my grandmother he couldn't control as the ghost entered Bhagna's body appeared to be more powerful.

Then suggest somebody's name in or out of the locality who could empower the ghost and could throw him out for ever. - said my grandmother to his brother.

"It is only Haji Sultan Khan. He is the most powerful tantric living just in Tundi Road, Lal Bazar. He does 5 times namaj regularly and lives and leads a pure and pious life. God is always with him like shadow and protects him in all that he does for humanity." Butan Mian an associate of Hari Singh said very confidently.

Bisna! Go and bring him sharp. My grandmother said to Bisna.

Butan Mian held Bisna under his arms and said, " Didi! Please send Sitaram Babu, only then Haji Saheb will come."

My grandmother hinted his younger brother to run fast and bring him soon.

Sitaram Dada obeyed his elder sister. He left and brought Haji Saheb with him.

Haji Saheb marked my uncle's mood and mentality. He asked all the people to vacate the room as any unprecedented thing could happen any time. In fear the crowd went off the place.

Haji Saheb's grandson Abdul Sammad was my classmate and usually I visited his house for study. He was knowing me personally so he did not ask me to go out of the room.

Instead he said, "Beta! Tum palang par chadh jao, wahin se dekho."

I did so.

He brought some water in a pot and sprinkled around his body first. Then he asked my grandmother to bring some mustard oil in a pot.

He recited some mantras several times and exhaled his breath air every time over the mustard oil.

He peeped into the eyes of my uncle and asked some questions as to why he did so.
"Tell the truth otherwise I will close you in an empty bottle and throw you into the sea." He added. The ghost sat down at his feet and said, "This man made our dwelling place impure and nasty by urinating and evacuating. We keep our dwelling place quite neat and clean and pure in all respect. We can't tolerate a man or woman doing so, so I captured his whole body to teach him a lesson. We are ghosts but not so unkind or cruel like man that we take life. Now my very purpose is served and since you come and order me, I will leave him soon."

Haji Saheb heard all but he caught my uncle's hairs very tightly, caught his neck and poured the saudhik mustard oil into both his ears. My uncle cried out loudly in acute pain. He stood up and fled away. Haji Saheb warned all to let him go as far as possible. He added, " He is to fall down when the ghost leaves him and goes out of his body and mind".

A large number of spectators followed him and at last my uncle fell down on the Grand Trunk Road and became senseless.

Haji Saheb, my grandmother and myself came to him. Haji Saheb checked his pulse and the beating of his heart too.

He said to us, "Don't worry. Let him sleep. He will wake up himself after an hour or so. Till his sense returns, keep watch on him carefully."

I remained there along with my grandmother till my uncle opened his eyes.

My uncle sense came back and seeing around exclaimed with surprise, "Where am I and what has happened to me?"

"Let us go home first, then I will brief you what has happened." My grandmother said to him.

About six decades passed but still I remember the unprecedented incident that had happened in my boyhood.

****

Ambitious - How Much To Be

Short story is a statement of incidence or happening which is in short/brief and readers can finish it in a single sitting within the shortest possible time and can conclude what the theme is and what the writer wants to convey in sort of a message to the people of the society through it. Here are two short stories of two different parents of two different families.
First Family
Mr. Mallick was a good friend of mine. He was Dy. Chief Finance Manager in a PSU and mine was Finance Manager. We were working in the same department under the different controlling officers. Both of us were being controlled under staff and line management system. As such my CO was CMS of the hospital and GM (F) at HQ whereas his was GM (System) and GM (F) at HQ.GM(F) was the Head of the Finance in the company as whole. We had to attend the GM (F)'s and D (F)'s meetings at HQ as and when called for. He very often represented GM (System), his CO – HOD of Computer Department. Here also we met and talked about the working trend and policy of our company.

We discussed about the progress of work of the Areas including ours in his department.
My friend was very calm and quit. He was very intelligent and well behaved. Everybody loved him like anything. He was in charge of a section and assigned with very responsible job. Under him were working a good number of executives and nonexecutives as subordinates to assist him in discharging his duty efficiently and effectively.
I used to attend his office very frequently and had to see him about the work of my office. Very happily did he use to listen to my problem and used to order his subordinate to get the job done on priority basis as I was a good friend of him and posted in to take care of the officers, staff and workers of the hospital to their expectation.
Though Mr. Mallick was a good friend of mine, I never pressurized him for any job at any time. The ways I used to present my cases or grievances, immediately did he understand. Sometimes when he was extremely busy, our eyes were sufficient enough to understand each other.
Secondly his wife was Sr. Medical Officer in our hospital and I was the HOD and paying officer. Mrs. Mallick knows that I was the good friend of

his husband. My friend was worriless, since I was there to take care of her in all that she needed in connection with her pay, allowances and perks.

Mr. & Mrs. Mallick were living happily in a very good bungalow with her only daughter Miss Pratibha Mallick (name changed) who was not only beautiful as fairy but very intelligent student in an English Medium highly reputed school of the region also. She was topping in her classes almost all the years. We were expecting that today or tomorrow she would do something miracle in her life.

Here is a turning point in the short story:

Miss Pratibha Mallick passed tenth class with about 98% marks in science stream. She topped in her school. One and all concerned were very happy to congratulate the student for excellent performance in the board exam.and the parents too for right guidance to their daughter.

Parents were highly ambitious about her daughter taking into consideration her extraordinary result in tenth board. They thought of admitting her daughter in one of the most prestigious and highly reputed schools in New Delhi. Wife and husband consulted each other, talked to their near and dear ones and her daughter too and came to a conclusion to admit

her in New Delhi's as stated above. As I learnt from the reliable sources that the principal of the school requested Mr. and Mrs. Mallick not to take her daughter anywhere, keep her there itself, she would do the best in twelfth and could compete any JEE of the country, but the parents turned a deaf ear to her request, instead took the TC along with all necessary certificates and testimonials to facilitate her admission in New Delhi.
They rushed to New Delhi and admitted her daughter in a very prestigious and highly reputed school and after leaving her in school's hostel came back happily to their bungalow.

Mr. and Mrs. Mallick returned happily after admitting her daughter in New Delhi's school. They bought almost all things her daughter wanted from them while leaving her in the hostel. Everything was settled so nicely that the parents as well as their daughter looked extremely happy.
Whosoever asked from them about their daughter, they replied that she was alright there and doing well.
Every day at night they used to talk to their daughter over telephone by turn about how she

was pulling on. She said, "Everything is OK, nothing to worry at all.

Days were passing on their flying wings as pleasantly as in Fairy Tales.
"Now we are free from one anxiety – about the career of our daughter, she is in one of the best schools of New Delhi, no worry about her higher education, she can compete any joint entrance examination after twelfth, no doubt in it."- Parents were so confident that they used to say to their friends.
The parents whenever got time proceeded to New Delhi to see their daughter also. So much love and affection they showered till they lived with their daughter that while departing with the daughter their eyes were filled with tears, they had to hold them inside. With sheer smile on the faces they saw off the daughter at the hostel gate.

Here is the turning point in the story.

I was extremely engaged in auditing of books of accounts in the office. The statutory auditors were sitting in front of my table and busy in work. It was about eleven O'clock in the morning. Just then Mazumdar Babu, Accountant entered my chamber and to his utter surprise said to me, "Do you know, Sir! A very sad news!"

What has happened? Tell me clearly.

You know Mr. Malik's daughter?

Yes.
She was reading in New Delhi.

I know it also. What has happened, tell me.

She is no more.

How? She was alright. What happened and how died?
She committed suicide, she was found dead in her hostel room. Just now I received the news over telephone from Mr. Sinha, one of my friends in Head Quarter.

We were stunned to get this sad news. The auditors stood up and stopped the work. I said to Mazumdar Babu, "Let us go to his bungalow." We rushed there and the scene we came across was very tragic. A large number of well-wishers were in and around the bungalow. Mrs. Mallick was senseless to hear the sad news and admitted to hospital. Mr. Mallick was surrounded by his colleagues who were consoling him but it had no effect on Mr. Malik's mind. He was at a loss to decide what to do then, no charm in life, everything gone!

He cried bitterly since he heard the sad news, his was not ready to believe in the news. His eyes were dried up, no tears to shed any longer. What he thought of and what happened, now what for his life was, meaningless without her, how and why occurred, what wrong he had committed in life that he was punished so cruelly by God...

Too many mouths, too many comments. Someone said, "Mr. Mallick should not have withdrawn her daughter from here. She was doing well here, not at all necessary to admit her to New Delhi's school.

Another commented, "New Delhi is not a good place for us. Students from different states join the school and one is jealous of another, can do harm to anyone."

Mr. Mazumdar asked me, "Sir! What is your opinion about Mr. Malik's decision?"

In my opinion it was a wrong decision to withdraw the daughter and admit her to New Delhi's school. Mr. and Mrs. Mallick shouldn't have become overambitious about their daughter."

"Only one daughter the parents have, they should not have kept her far away from their eyes." – One of his colleagues gave his views. "Very unfortunate!"- said D (F) and asked his secretary to extend all co-operation and assistance to Mr. Malik's family.

"Let the situation be normal, we have decided to proceed to New Delhi today. We want to see the Principal and want to know actually what has happened and why?"- One of the Malik's relatives said to us.

One by one the people left with the heavy hearts, only a few were present there to take care of Mr. Mallick, his wife and other kith and kin.
So many things appeared and disappeared in my mind one by one, the whole matters from beginning to the end before my eyes, I could not come to conclusion what fault was there either with the parents or her daughter that resulted in such an unfortunate end.

I think till now you might have gone through the first story. In this story the parents were overambitious about their daughter. The school where she studied from nursery to class ten was in no way lower than any highly reputed school, but even then the parents withdrew their daughter and admitted her to New Delhi's school in anticipation that she would perform the best beyond imagination which can help build her career excellently after twelfth. Here the daughter was attending her school in the morning by school bus and coming back in the afternoon every day. The parents loved her like anything and the daughter also love her parents immensely. With the sunrise their love and affection starts with but even late in night it continues till the daughter did not go to bed and sleep well. She was in well guidance and supervision of their parents, so to say under their eyelids whereas in New Delhi she was far - far away from the sight of her parents.

Whatsoever the reasons might be, the story ended in tragedy, resulting in unbearable loss to the family of Mr. Mallik.

The second story is just reverse of that i.e. the first one.

Shashikant was a student of class ten in a village High School. He passed tenth class with very good marks. His parents were very pleased with the result of their son. There were many options for admission of the boy. Someone advised to admit him to Saint Xavier College, Ranchi, some to Saint Columbus College, Hazaribagh, some asked father to admit him to New Delhi's school. Father heard everyone patiently, did not displease any one by opposing face to face.
The parents were of the opinion not to send their eldest son anywhere, but to admit him to a local college.

One day father called his son and wanted to know his view also. His son replied briefly, "What you think is acceptable to me. I will do better irrespective of what of standard college is."

The college was only eight kilometres from his house. He used to attend his classes regularly. His father sat with him, asked how he was pulling on, how his classes were held, regularly or irregularly, so many things were discussed between the son and the father.

As soon as the boy passed twelfth class, he was admitted to the same college.
The boy expressed his desire to take B.Sc. (Hons.) in Mathematics.
Father said to him clearly, "If you be a school master, I will be the happiest person, I have the least desire, you must too, but work so sincerely, so hard that you can compete one of the toughest entrance examination of the country, side by side you will have to plan properly and prepare for both the examinations at the same time. I know you will have to work very hard, what of that, one day it will repay you, and you will forget what you sacrifice now. We are here, myself, your mother, your elder sister, your younger brothers – all will help you in your study as well as in your sports and games which you like to play after you feel monotony and be free from your study. You can relax whenever you are tired of work."

When the boy passed B.SC. (Hons) in Math. Part – I Exam and obtained 89% in Math., the highest marks in the college, his father asked him what entrance examination he wanted to prepare then. His son replied he would prepare for IIT only. "O.K.", - his father nodded his head.

"Well! As books are the best teachers, I can buy necessary books for you. Make efforts from your end to get all necessary syllabus, question papers etc. for the last few years or so. By that time I am registering your name as an external student to Brilliant Tutorials, Chennai - one year postal coaching, it will help you and guide you to a great extent for preparation. You can join three teachers for three different subjects for tuition also. The names that you have proposed are of high repute, so I allow you."- His father said to him.

The boy himself sought for a lonely place in the house for study. It was in first floor. Mother used to go there with a glass of milk or Horlicks every morning and evening.

In B.Sc. second year he obtained 78% marks in honours papers.
He appeared in IIT JEE but not competed when he was in second year. He didn't lose heart and once again appeared when he was in final year of B.SC.(Hons.)

This year he was selected for admission to IIT, Kharagpur. His AIR was around 1500.
Here is the Turning Point in the story.
He studied for 4 years, selected in campus and joined an MNC. He guided his younger brothers, helped them financially in their admission to engineering colleges. When his father retired from services of the company, he took the whole charge on his shoulder and made the parents free from household anxiety.

The son works in an MNC and holds a key post but far - far away from his father nearly 2000 kilometres from home - his native place. But not too far as the distance has shrunk to the nearest one with the development of science & technology in communication inasmuch as mobile, smartphone, internet, and video conferencing are readily available for whole day for use. The parents and the son talk to each other and share their views regularly.
When the son arrives home, father goes one step forward and embraces his son with love and affection that he deserves.
My dear friends!
Now you have read both the stories. No doubt in it when we are overambitious, we will have to pay for it. And when we think of the least, exert

utmost for the best, there are favourable chances that we can pave the way to achieve our goal.

✶✶✶✶✶✶✶✶✶✶✶✶✶✶✶✶✶✶✶✶✶✶✶✶✶✶✶✶✶✶✶✶✶✶✶✶

Turning Point

I was unaware of her name. I never tried to know it. It was not at all necessary.
One day I addressed her as Chandramukhi. She stared at me and to her utter surprise she said, "How did you know my name?"
Your face is just like the full Moon, that is why I …
O, I see!
Moreover your face is round as the full Moon and it is as beautiful as …
Some shades are also there as that of the moon.
Lovely one, pretty one, attractive too!
What does "attractive" mean?
Attractive means to attract the people towards your face – means to say towards you.
I am a woman. I understand everything. On the very first day I understood as to why you stare at me, why you talk to me unnecessarily, why you stay for a long time in front of me.
For instance yesterday you came to give me the washed shirts and pants for ironing but you started putting so many questions such as when I was married, to whom I was married, what my husband was doing, how old I was and he… so

on.

Nonsense! So many questions at a time, even my husband does not ask from me, why you? With so many queries you kept me engaged, by that time I could have ironed at least 15 clothes.

How much you have lost, may be forty five rupees, I will make it up by paying it to you. Why should I take it from you? When I didn't do anything. Should I accept any consideration for no work?

On the first day I told you that we run this laundry, its name is Ramchandran Laundry after my husband's name.

I love my husband and my husband loves me too.

Have I ever asked you how much you love your husband and how much your husband … so irrelevant? When you say irrelevant, doesn't it matter? When I do, it pinches you. Doesn't it? Forget all that has happened till now in between you and I. From the next day please don't come, send your son instead.

OK. I said to her and left her laundry immediately.

I used to go for shopping every morning and evening by her laundry but I passed straight. I never turned my eyes towards her laundry. I heard her chirping but I turned a deaf ear to it. I was quite careless whether she was looking at me or not. What I wanted was that that she should come forward first to talk to me, she should surrender and ask apology for what she did with me.

Four days passed smoothly but on the fifth day my anxiety to see her was multiplied. I prayed to God to keep my prestige at all cost.

If anyone prays to God sincerely with true devotion and dedication, God hears patiently and helps him/her.

On the fifth day in the evening I was crossing the path of her laundry, she rushed and stopped my way to go forward, she caught hold of my right hand strongly and dragged to her laundry and said:

Since last four days your son didn't come here to give clothes, what is the matter?

The matter is crystal clear, I asked him not to go and not to give you any clothes.

Why?

I want to see how many days you keep yourself without talking to me. Just like the promise of Gangaram.

What does it mean?

Gangaram was an innocent boy. While playing with a ball, he entered the campus of a University. He entered the chamber of the Vice

Chancellor which was open and none was present there. He saw a beautiful chair. It was a revolving chair. He sat in it and started rocking. He was moving right, then left and was enjoying sitting in it. Just then the Vice Chancellor entered and seeing the boy rocking in his chair, he became extremely angry. He slapped on his cheeks, twisted his ears, scolded him and dragged him out.

The boy stared at the Vice Chancellor and felt so insulted that he promised that he would study sincerely, would work hard, would leave no stone unturned and would become Vice Chancellor and would sit in that chair one day or other.

As the insult touched his sentiment, he studied day and night, passed almost all examinations with distinction. The day came when he became the Vice Chancellor of the University and sat in the chair. Thus he fulfilled his promise. It was said to be " Gangaram Ki Tek. "

Very inspiring story. So you too promised not to see me unless or until I call you first. You fulfilled your promise and looked extremely pleased. Isn't it?

Of course! The way you asked me not to come pinched me bitterly and I promised I wouldn't see you unless or until you call me first.

What I realised very seriously while passing through my laundry, you never turned even your neck towards me as if you were hating to look at me. So much hatred, so much revenge for such a trifle matter you were giving that I could not have sound sleep at night even when I started thinking about your berookhi (declination). Whole day I remained mentally disturbed, unwilling to do any work, so I told everything to my husband who advised me to stop your ways and to drag you to the laundry, I had no alternative but to act accordingly. Now you are standing before me as an accused. I will deliver order for fine or imprisonment. Do as deems fit, I have no objection. Do come every morning, every evening without gap, understand.

When I see you, when I talk to you, something – something pleasant I feel within my heart as well as in my mind.

It is nothing but love of a woman towards a man. Here you are a woman and I am a man and love has taken place in between you and I. Isn't it?

Of course! But it is not fair. There is some exceptional moment in one's life when he or she falls in love with someone though it must not be as in case of a married woman loving another man. It is against social ethics but people go beyond it.

She listened to me attentively but kept silent. Didn't utter anything either in favour or in against. I also closed the topic here.

She called a boy working in a garage and asked him to fetch two cups of tea. The boy rushed to and brought tea for us.

We were seeping as slowly as could be and with each seep staring at each other, we were observing silence.

Eyes have their own language. We were talking to each other in that language.

As it was too late, I turned round to leave her alone. I after stepping a few yards turned back and noticed she was standing as statue at the same place where I had left her.

Woman's heart is naturally very tender just like the petals of rose flowers. We have to nourish it time to time otherwise it may fade away soon. Woman cannot conceal or hide the feeling that she realizes in heart or mind, naturally it glows on her face that one can read easily. When she is happy, her happiness glows on her face, on the contrary when she is worried, anxiety defaces her.

God has created woman for man and has done a great thing for him otherwise …? What would have happened is beyond my imagination. Alas! We could have understood His philosophy! How foolish we are, even then we do not pay due regard and respect to the women we live and lead with in every walk of our life – here, there and everywhere!

I came back to my house and noticed that a number of washed clothes were lying for ironing in two bags. Next day as usual at ten in the morning I took these bags and came to the laundry. Chandramukhi was not there in the laundry in her place some aged person was at the front table and was ironing the clothes. He was bald headed and looked about 40/ 41 years of age. Only some hairs were in black and white mixed on the lower parts of his head all around. His face was well maintained with modern cosmetics to conceal his oldness that appeared at the first sight any one could see.

I asked him, "Where is your daughter, Chandramukhi? I am not seeing her."

She is my wife, not daughter. Her name is Rajlakshmi, not Chandramukhi.

I address her as Chandramukhi as her face resembles with the moon – full Moon.

I don't mind whatever the name you call her. What's the matter? Tell me, I will help you. Some clothes are herein these two bags – already washed by us. Please iron them and keep ready for delivery tomorrow at ten in the morning. I

will come to collect myself.
Today my wife has some urgent work at home. Tomorrow she must be here.
Well, One thing I want to know your wife looks so young about twenty years old whereas you about forty...
Not forty, I am forty five years old.
Then how did you manage the marriage? How did her parents agree? Didn't the girl, now your wife object it?
In fact the girl, my wife didn't object it provided I could agree to her only one
condition. Moreover her father was no more. Her mother worked as a maid servant in some nearby houses, her financial condition was very wretched. The young boys of the locality teased her now and then, anything could happen with her, kidnapping, rape and so on. Mine is very sound and I am the only son of my parents. My father expired long back. My old mother and my elder sister wanted me to settle in life but every time I put some excuses before them. In fact I fell into a bad company, used to attend night clubs, bar houses, hotels and even red areas, with all these unfair ways of life I was addicted to drinking and smoking which ultimately resulted in chest problem and on diagnosis the physician told me that I suffered from tuberculosis and I

needed proper treatments for at least one year, and I will have to give up all these bad habits if I wanted to survive, otherwise…

It was the turning point in my life. In fact I didn't want to die, I wanted to please my mother and my elder sister fulfilling their desire to marry and settle in life. In the heart of the city I own a big market complex from where I get Rs.50000 as rent every month. My Jeejaji and the elder sister took care of me, admitted me to a very good hospital cum sanatorium and within a very short period of time in eight months I was totally recovered and my health also improved with nutritious and balance diets and the environment I was living in. I repented over my past life that I led in a bad company and promised to live a simple life.

I heard all about your past life as well as the present one but one important matter still remains unanswered.

What's that?

That is the condition that was put up to you for marriage by your wife, Chandramukhi.

Unbelievable! But even then I don't hesitate to disclose it to you.

She told me sincerely that she had had a boyfriend whom she loved most since her childhood and in turn the boy loved her most too. The boy as belonged to a Brahmin family and she to a scheduled caste, marriage couldn't be materialized at any cost, if any one dared so, none would be spared , they would be cut into pieces by someone who opposed such inter caste marriage and…..?

Then what did you do ultimately?

I had to accept her condition ultimately as there was no way out for me, I, though recovered from tuberculosis, looked like an old man.

The terms and conditions were more or less bearable under the situations I was living without wife, truly speaking without settling in life.

I agreed with her to the terms and conditions laid down before me for marriage.

Could I know the terms and conditions?

Why not? She would live with me for six days – Monday to Saturday and only one day on every Sunday for 24 hours she would be with her boyfriend and would come back to join him at ten in the next morning i.e. on every Monday. She added further she would be a faithful wife and would serve me wholeheartedly, I could enjoy with her as I liked constructively for six days but for one day in a week I must not envy rather I must co-operate them without any hitch. I approved it.

The moment I talked to my brother-in-law and my elder sister, they rushed to my house and talked to my mother whose joy knew no bound to learn my desire to marry. Accordingly a thorough search was made for a suitable bride for me and within a week's time I was married to Rajlakshmi.

We after marriage went to Goa for honeymoon. We stayed for five days and enjoyed our conjugal life to the extreme. She co-operated in all that I deserved to do in such an occasion.

We came back and everything was normal. We were following the terms and the conditions in right spirit and letters.

"Rajlakshmi is as sincere and obedient as any good wife of a good family. She doesn't conceal anything from me. I too"- he added.

She was happy to state to me every Monday night how she spent her long awaited moment with her boyfriend in day as well as at night under his arms. She didn't hesitate to explain that that was as sweet as she spent with me almost the whole week in day and at night. She added she didn't feel any difference between us – me and her boyfriend. That was why I not only loved her but paid due respect from the core of my heart also.

"Let us take your matter. You give her two

toffees every morning. She keeps them intact. While going to bed, she tells everything about you – word by word and shares the toffees with me. We enjoy together even the trifle things that happen between you and my wife. "- he said to me.

I said to him, "Truly speaking I never thought of it. It appears unbelievable to me. What strong will power and courage she has been blessed with ! Amazing! I have never heard or read about such a unique character anywhere or in any book. I can say she is superb. You are the most fortunate husband.

She is a great fan to you and always in a fresh mood while leaving the house in the morning for the laundry. If such affair of love and affection prolongs for a longer period, I am afraid she may flee away with you somewhere.

Mr.Ramchandran! I am about seventy years old, have grandsons and granddaughters of your wife's age, can she do it? Never. Since morning as I see you haven't found any foolish person to cut such a foolish joke.

Sir! You are well aware of the fact that she doesn't see the age of a person but see his internal quality i.e. fairness and frankness in behaviour.

"Truth is truth and if there is any substitute of

truth, it is the truth only, nothing else."- He added.
Rajlakshmi!
Not Rajlakshmi, it is Chandramukhi , the name you have given to her and you always address her while talking to for hours together.
Be free from my side ...
What? Intervened Mr. Ramchandran.
I am not kidnapping your good wife. She is with you and will be with you whole life as a sincere better half. Don't be confused nor did you confuse me in the matter in question. It is now too late, most probably my wife has been waiting anxiously for me.
At least let us take tea together. He asked Tenia to rush and bring two cups of tea. After taking tea, I stepped down and reached house. While stepping down, Mr. Ramchandran said addressing me, "Sir! Please do come tomorrow morning, she will be here positively, as I will be out of station, in fact I will be going to Mysore to see my elder sister who has been suffering from jaundice. Do come and also take away your clothes, will be ready by that time.
"What were you doing for such a long time? I find you are taking too much interest in the baby, that young lady."- my wife standing at the gate and waiting for me asked.

Today she was not there, her husband was, he kept me engaged, what could I do? We forgot the time while talking about some important topic.

"I know you and your topic since …?"- My wife added.

Well then!

Come with me tomorrow and see the young baby and her attachment with me too with your open eyes and ears. Mera mood kharab mat karo (Don't disturb my mood), I am tired of too much shopping, totally exhausted.

Getting a light dose, my wife's temperature became normal. She brought warm water to wash my legs, hands and face. I switched on the TV and concentrated on the national news.

Next morning at ten as usual I took two bags – one full of washed clothes and another to bring the washed ones.

I saw Chandramukhi awaiting from a long distance. As I stood before her counter, she stretched her eyes, looked at my face, tried to read something from it and annoyingly asked, " What did you say to my husband about me?"

So many things, what of that?

Didn't your husband tell you about the discussion we made about you?

Take your washed clothes, give me another ones.

Where are my toffees?
This time better, five star.
How much spent?
Twenty only, ten rupees each.
Why?
Ask your husband, he can better reply.
OK
Now it is my turn to ask you who that handsome boy was who dropped you from his bike.
My boyfriend, Venugopal. We love each other since our childhood.
Then why didn't you marry?
He belongs to Brahmin caste whereas I scheduled caste. Our marriage cannot be materialized, if we do so, we wouldn't be spared, will be cut into pieces.
Then how?
I married Ramchandran conditionally.
What conditions?
I will spend every Sunday whole day and whole night with Venu as couple. This relaxation has been gladly granted by my husband.
No ways out for him, he has no alternative but to accept the conditions. Just see he sleeps with me consecutively for six days and night, he smashes me as he likes, I never object, tolerate everything as a good wife. In case I spend only one night in a week with Venu, why should he think

otherwise?

I also made it clear that we know each other's past history and about you all know what you were and how you were indulged in bad habits.

I asked a question from her, '' Have you tried to know the changes in the face of your husband when you resume him on the next day and night on Monday? ''

Woman is blessed with an inborn quality that she can know the matter of the heart and head merely peeping into man's eyes. Have you ever realised any time, any moment that your husband doesn't want you to loiter here and there and spend the night with him as wife. I am of the opinion that no husband wants that his wife should sleep with another man.

One year has passed peacefully, everything is normal, never complained rather was happy to see us together, in many occasions we saw the movie, had the dinner in hotels and restaurants, we enjoyed together friends alike. But since last two or three weeks I find him in agony, if I ask anything, he instead of replying is lost somewhere... I can't say how it has happened all of a sudden and for what?

Chandramukhi! I'm sure he is under depression. Anything may happen any time.

What type of disease it is?

I can't explain exactly but it is a kind of mental pressure or depression when a person loses control over mind.
I suggest you to consult a psychiatric.
What changes did you find in his ways of action of behaviour?
Last Monday at about ten in the morning Venu dropped me at the doorstep. As I entered the bedroom, I found him in deep sleep, most of the things were lying scattered, one empty wine bottle was on the table, two glasses , one empty and another full of water were near the bottle. A half burnt candle was on the plate. Under the centre table cigarette pieces were also seen. He has already given up drinking and smoking, then what caused him to restart them to take. I was very nervous. I called the maid servant who apprised me of the whole things, he couldn't sleep at night, thinking something irrelevant and took wine and cigarette.
When I aroused him, he started confusing me with unusual talks i.e. how we spent the night, what we took in dinner at Savoy etc. He concealed what exactly happened and why?
I also guessed that he was feeling guilty of what he did at night in her absence, he wanted to veil the truth.
Whatever you say, how much more you believe

in your husband, I am sanguine that he didn't like you to accompany another man, be your boyfriend,to spend the night with him. Chandramukhi! Not a good sign, I am afraid of any unusual consequences, can happen on ant day at any time. It is my apprehension but logical.
Please listen to me patiently. A husband can excuse his wife in so many matters but not that you have been committing for a year. He may be a very gentle man but in this issue he may lose his temper, even peace of his mind, can do anything undesirable under depression. I know many such cases where conjugal life was either disturbed or came to an end.
If you want to lead a happy conjugal life, you will have to leave Venu, no other ways I see except this.
She became sad to hear my advice. Gathering courage she told that she was ready to face the situations and circumstances whatsoever they might be, but at any cost she couldn't depart with Venu, let the sky fall over her head, she didn't bother for that.
I don't care for the consequences I will have to face in the years to come. Venu and I will not do anything undesirable or unpleasant but if my husband does anything wrong, he will be held

responsible for it. We can't help. He can murder Venu, he can poison me also or both, we are ready to face any consequences, any, even death, clearly telling you, Sir!
The consequences are crystal clear. Your husband can arrange to kill Venu, but he will not do it.
Why?
Because your husband knows that you cannot live without him, you may commit suicide in case Venu is murdered.
He will not kill you.
Why?
Because he loves most, he cannot live without you.
Then what can my husband do you are apprehending to ?
Only one alternative is left out for him.
May I Know it?
He will kill himself this way or that way sooner or later.
What do you mean to say?
I mean to say that either he will suit himself or hang with and commit suicide.
He knows it and many a time he has seen both of you how acutely you stare at each other, how impatiently you embrace each other, how deeply you kiss each other, nothing is hidden now from

his eyes. His eyes are broadened when he looks at such an unusual thing. He smiles while talking but does not mean he is happy with you.
He also knows that you can live and lead your live even he shoots himself dead or commits suicide by hanging.
Are you sure?
Of course!
Human beings are governed by their past good or bad things that he/she has done. Here yours have been repenting over his past sins that he did in bad company. His soul is cursing him every now and then. He is in immense strain and stress, in fact in depression.
Chandrmukhi looked disappointed. I was so tired of talking the irrelevant things unnecessarily for a long time that after taking coffee in the tea stall I left for house.
My son said to me, " Babuji! You have taken much more time in returning from the laundry.
Discussing some important issues
Whom?
Chandramukhi and his family.
Don't involve yourself unnecessarily in this city. Everybody has got the family problems, we have too, what can we do for others? No time to think about?
You are right, even then we are not concerned at

all and must not be, but as a social animal and as a part of the society, if any member is in trouble, what is the harm in sharing the problem?

I am seventy years old, have bitter experience of conjugal life and the differences arising out of lack of trust between the husband and wife. If I suggest anything that can settle the issue, I think it will also be a sort of service to the needy people like Chandramukhi, his husband and moreover his boyfriend.

O.K. My son informed that he has arranged our going back home next Monday by Go Airways direct from Bengaluru to Kolkata in the afternoon flight.

Thank you. Well done!

We are very happy that you are satisfied with the treatment here in St. John Hospital and going back quite well.

We stayed here for a month but how our days passed we could not know.

May I know what attracted you most?

Its climate, neither cold nor hot, no pollution. City is almost neat and clean. People are badly engaged in their work – all the five, six days. They enjoy Sunday somewhere in park, zoo, lake, gardens, temples etc. with their family. We visited ISKON temple, very good arrangement for the visitors. Lal Bagh is also worth visiting.

Lord Shiva Temple, Sai Temple, Halsuru Lake, administration, law and order, wide roads, well managed traffic – all round the city. Here a large number of software companies – national and international have their offices where the engineers and non-engineers are employed. They are from the different regions of the states of the country.
If you like so, why don't you shift here from house ?
Not practicable now for us, as we have so many engagements and commitments there, our native place where born and brought up, our near and dear ones we have been living with, so cannot shift permanently.
OK.
Every day I used to take and bring the clothes from the laundry and used to stay for a few minutes and talk either to Chandramukhi or to her husband – Ramchandran.
I noticed that she was sad- quite calm and quit, worried so much while replying my questions Which I asked in course of talking- that was unwillingly too.
What has happened to you, tell me openly, possibly I can do something for you.
"Face indicates of mind. Your face has faded, no charms, your eyes are reddish. I don't find you

in a cheerful mood."- I said to her.
She disclosed that that on the last Friday night he was so annoyed that he didn't wish me as doing earlier rather dragged the chair in anger and sat in front of me – eyes to eyes he said to me,
"Listen to me patiently. I do not want you to go with Venu henceforth, the reasons are very clear, the people are jeering at me, saying that I am impotent, no control over my wife, leaving her to spend the night with her boyfriend.
I love you most. It's true that what I say to you to follow is against the terms and conditions agreed by both us before marriage, but now I am not in a position to adhere to it.
It is my earnest request for the sake of God, forget Venu for ever. Let me live a peaceful conjugal life.
I was more shocked than surprised to hear it, no ways out to argue, I said to him I would think over this issue, please allow me some time.
Decide within 24 hours by Saturday night and apprise me of your opinion, must not be later than this.
Chandramukhi! I am merely your customer, nothing to take and give, since I come every day, talk to every day, a relation has developed between us, we may call it love, but we must not take it otherwise.

"I never think otherwise about you even in dream you are so nice, a gentleman, an ideal person… ?"- She said to me.

"Chandramukhi! I have sympathy not only for you, but for your husband- Ramchandran, and over and above your boyfriend- Venugopal also. You are very wise, know about the pros and cons of the total issue better than me. I can ask you only to settle the issue amicably, please don't delay otherwise you will have to pay for it, you will have to…?

Chandramukhi! It is for information that I will be leaving for home next Monday afternoon by flight, tickets are confirmed. Do not know when we will be meeting once again in Bengaluru."- I added.

On Saturday evening I brought all the clothes and on Sunday I didn't go as I was extremely busy in packing our luggage.

My wife was also with me. We came to Bengaluru for our routine health check – up in St. John Hospital College.

It is said that another story starts with the story that the writer wants to say primarily, same was the case with me, not irrelevant to tell here.

People are of the view that men are of doubtful nature, but truly speaking women are more than men.

My dear readers! One day my wife asked me, " So near the laundry is situated, what's the reason every day you are coming late, sometimes very late after one or two hours, what are you doing there? I am afraid you are entangled somewhere with somebody – must be a woman.

You are right, she is a woman I am entangled with. I confess it.

Please accompany me today evening, see with your own eyes the whole…?

As stated I along with my wife came to the laundry. Chandramukhi was there at the counter and engaged in ironing clothes. She stopped the work and wished us as usual. I introduced my wife. She bid pranaam folding her hands.

I gave her two toffees.

I ask my wife to know the reasons as to why I was late every day.

Jokingly I said, "We have already decided to flee away from here to Nepal and settle there.

Aunty! Don't believe uncle, he always jokes like this. We were talking together about family affairs, he was advising me what to do and what not to do, by that time I was making his clothes ready, we were also taking tea.

Aunty! Uncle is a gentle man, by heart he is very kind to everybody. He talks so friendly as if he were own relative. My husband also takes

interest in talking to him. He is of the opinion that uncle is very clean by heart, whatever he says, says from the core of his heart. When uncle and my husband discusses about any issue, it is too difficult to understand who keeps more engaged – uncle or my husband. They go on talking and discussing hours together.
Aunty! Uncle addresses me as Chandrakuhki whreas my name is Rajlakshmi. With so much love and affection he calls me by name that we don't object rather we are lost somewhere for a few seconds.
Aunty! Uncle has got the enchanting power, anybody can be attracted towards him when he talks to.
Uncle knows how to hypnotize a person, he is versed in this art.
My wife was convinced about our relation and also came to know as to why I was late every day.
We took tea and went to market for shopping. We came back to our house shortly.
In the evening we came out for evening walk to Halsuru Lake. I said to my wife to see Chandramukhi in return inasmuch as it would be our last meeting. She agreed and we came to her laundry, saw she was at the counter doing the job of ironing the clothes.

She welcomed us and requested to sit down inside the room. We were standing before the counter. She asked the boy to bring three cups of tea. He asked my wife about her health. She said she had been suffering from blood pressure and blood sugar. She after treatment in St. John Hospital, was alright.

I said I had to undergo bypass surgery in 2002. Dr.Manoj J. Pradhan operated me so nicely that till now my heart is as good as of a healthy young man. I have been taking medicines since 2002 regularly and now quite healthy and fit. Besides medicines he has advised me to be good at work and to do good to the needy people of the society. The booklet that he had given me summarizes some advices for heart patients:

Eat a heart- healthy diet – low fat sources of protein
Do not smoke
Maintain a healthy weight
Exercise and Yoga
Salt restricted Diet
Work well, sleep well
Keep away from stress & strain
Be good and do good.

Another important thing for a heart patient is the laughter that everyone should do in order to keep fit and cheerful.

We after taking tea together left quickly as we had to arrange luggage.
We had to leave on Monday after noon. We were purchasing two newspapers – one in Hindi and another in English.
After taking tea and biscuits I took the paper in my hand to read. I read the headlines in the front page and turned the next page. I was more shocked than surprised to read, "A man committed suicide by hanging. " It was Ramchandran, husband of Chandramukhi who had committed suicide hanging by the fan in the bed room. We rushed to the spot of occurrence. We saw the people in a large number in front of the house talking about the incidence. We went inside the room and noticed Chandramukhi quite calm and quit surrounded by her well-wishers. We saw each other but she was not in a position to talk to us at that moment. The maid servant apprised us of how and when the incidence took place and why. It was early in the morning when she took the tea as usual, the door was closed from inside, no response was coming out even after calling again and again, knocking the door hard. She informed the people living nearby. The door was broken open. Ramchandran was hanging by the fan. He was taken down but the body was as cold as ice, he was dead. By that

time the doctor was called for who declared him dead.

My wife said to me, " Console Chandramukhi, she will listen to you. "

I said to her, "Bear the loss courageously, no way out now to repent over the past, it is the time to make all arrangements for his last rites properly, it is you who can do it, don't be nervous, don't think he would return if you give your life this way. We people are helpless, puppets in the hands of God, nothing can be done against His will.

The moment she heard me, she burst into tears and said, "I am the culprit and responsible for his death. I didn't listen to him nor did I yours.

The maid servant gave me the suicidal note which read as follows:

Dear Rajlakshmi,

I love you most and will be loving most. Truly speaking I was mentally disturbed under the situations and circumstances I was living without you , let it be for a day on Sunday, I was remembering you and missing you, particularly at night, loneliness was biting me and started thinking about some unusual things, to shoot Venu, to strangulate you to death, but I found it unjustified.

I know you love Venu and cannot depart with

him at any cost. I thought again and again and came to a conclusion better to end my life, so I prefer to commit suicide by hanging.
I have committed many sins in my life and one of them was marrying you knowing everything about your love with Venu.
I have requested Pradhan to allow you both to marry happily and lead a happy life.
I have requested my family advocate to arrange court marriage for you at any time you like. It is my last wish to be fulfilled by you earnestly before I breathe my last.
At last I make it clear that I am going to commit suicide willingly, nobody is behind it, nobody should be held responsible for it.
Yours lovingly,
Ramchandran.
Whosoever was present there was so emotional that their eyes were filled with tears – about to burst into.
We left with the permission of the family members.
We reached the airport well in time. The plane took off the ground and flying thirty thousand feet above the sea level.
I was very sad.
My wife looking at my face and marking the sadness on my face, said, " Why are you so sad?

It happened so, so with the wishes of God, none could stop it. With the pace of time everything will be normal, it is go of the world.

We took tea and by that time we were reaching Kolkata as the air hostess asked us to tie up the belt as the plane was about to land within a few minutes.

As we got down and were stepping forward, my wife realized my feeling and said to me like a philosopher, "Whatever has happened to Chandramukhi, it's unfortunate but no need to worry at all, everything is set right with the pace of time. Nobody is responsible for the incidence that has happened all of a sudden. It is a "Turning Point" in Chandramukhi's life. Feel free and forget it.

****

www.ingramcontent.com/pod-product-compliance
Lightning Source LLC
Chambersburg PA
CBHW070328190526
45169CB00005B/1793